· *Great Ideas For* ·

BUTTONS, BEADS, RIBBONS, AND LACE

· Great Ideas For ·

BUTTONS, BEADS, RIBBONS, AND LACE

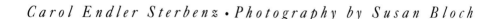

Carol Endler Sterbenz · Photography by Susan Bloch

CRESCENT BOOKS
NEW YORK ● AVENEL, NEW JERSEY

A FRIEDMAN GROUP BOOK

This 1994 edition published by Crescent Books, distributed by Outlet Book Company, Inc., a Random House Company,
40 Engelhard Avenue, Avenel, New Jersey 07001.

Random House
New York ● Toronto ● London ● Sydney ● Auckland

ISBN 0-517-10302-8

SIMPLY SENSATIONAL:
GREAT IDEAS FOR
BUTTONS, BEADS, RIBBONS, AND LACE
was prepared and produced by
Michael Friedman Publishing Group, Inc.
15 West 26th Street
New York, New York 10010

Editor: Elizabeth Viscott Sullivan
Designer: Tanya Ross-Hughes
Art Director: Jeff Batzli
Photography Editor: Christopher C. Bain
Illustrations: Kathy Bray

Color separations by Rainbow Graphic Arts Co., Ltd.
Printed and bound in China by Leefung-Asco Printers Ltd.

8 7 6 5 4 3 2 1

Every effort has been made to present the information in this book in a clear, complete, and accurate manner. It is important that all instructions be carefully followed, as failure to do so could result in injury, and the publisher and the author expressly disclaim any and all liability resulting therefrom.

For Rodney T. Sterbenz III

ACKNOWLEDGMENTS

For opening their button boxes to me, I wish to thank Grandma Endler and Grandma Sterbenz, and particularly Eileen Friedman, who shared the beautiful collection begun by her grandmother Molly and her mother, Ruth.

For her fabulous designs and inspiring ideas, and the many close moments shared in the creative process, I wish to thank my daughter Genevieve Aimee.

For her wisdom and support, I wish to thank my assistant, Nancy Johnson.

I wish to thank the following companies for their generous contribution of merchandise: Ellie Schneider and Katherine Horton of C.M. Offray and Son, Inc., for their beautiful ribbons; Larry Ash and David J. Schoenfarber of Streamline Industries, Inc., for their unique and beautiful buttons; Jill Novak of Levi Strauss and Company, for the denim jacket and jeans; Tara Gaffney of Capezio Ballet Makers, for the exercise wear; and Sarah Patterson and Maureen Maguire of Liz Claiborne, Inc., for the scarf.

I wish to extend particular thanks to several Long Island, New York merchants whose assistance made the styling of the photography possible: Melinda Fischer of Melinda's of Huntington, for loaning beautiful jewelry; Marilyn Bogdan and Irene Ciringione of Summer Stock, Montauk, for loaning lovely clothing; Dave and Adolphe Aebisher of Fort Hill Nursery, Huntington, for loaning plants and tools; and Don McCauley, Teresa Dickenson, and Irene Schmaltz, who opened every door of Spencer's Restaurant at the Town of Oyster Bay Golf Course in Woodbury for location photography.

Thanks also to Susan Bloch, photographer, and her assistant John Bentham, for the beautiful photography; to models Sherylann Kensington, Kristie Kovach, and Jeanne Bossolina; and to Genevieve Herr, for hair styling and makeup.

Finally, a special thank you to Elizabeth Sullivan, editor and friend extraordinaire, who inspired me every step of the way.

ntroduction
8

Notes on the Instructions in
This Book
10

Scoop-Neck Shell
With Ribbon Roses
12

V-Neck Shell With
Rose Necklace
15

Sweater With
Needlepoint Berries
18

Ribboned Bustier
With Folded Roses
22

Western Fringed Jacket
■
Beaded Shirt Collar
27

Vest With Star Constellations
and Beaded Tie
32

Beaded Top and
Bike Shorts
35

Faux Cuff Links
39

Faux Medals
39

Woven Evening Bag
∎
Button Earrings
43

Beaded Camisole and
Tap Pants
∎
Cropped Lace Jacket
∎
Satin Ribbon Pillow
∎
Cutwork Pillowcases
48

Sequin-Splashed
Opera Scarf
54

Blazer With Lace Trim
∎
Lapel Pin
57

Brass-Trimmed Blazer
60

Jeans With Lace Appliqués
63

Antique Lace Collar
66

Lace-Trimmed Nightgown
69

INTRODUCTION

Using ribbons, buttons, beads, lace, and other fashion trims to decorate clothing is one of the easiest, quickest, and least expensive ways to transform a wardrobe from so-so to sensational. With the mere addition of a well-placed bow or a dazzling button, it can be simple to modify or even dramatically alter the look of almost any article of clothing. You can expand the versatility of your wardrobe and express your personal style by searching no further than your own closets and drawers, and then—unless you are in the habit of collecting wonderful trims and buttons—visiting your local notions or trimmings shop.

In fact, your own closets and drawers are ideal places in which to look for apparel to revamp or decorate, as are the many mail-order catalogs that feature inexpensive basic garments. Most of the ideas in this book rely on the understanding that we all have items in our wardrobe that could use a lift; we all have a favorite piece of clothing that needs a little something to bring it up to date; and we all love basic pieces but want to individualize them without spending a fortune.

Drawing on your own wardrobe for clothing and accessories to decorate is a practical approach, but you also might want to try another terrific source: the vintage clothing shop. Vintage clothing shops sell a variety of apparel, accessories, and jewelry, and some even specialize in the styles of a particular era, such as the forties or fifties, or in a particular type of clothing, such as beaded sweaters or lingerie. Of course, each shop is unique, but in most shops you are likely to find racks of wonderful, and occasionally elegant, clothing—generally in gently used condition and at quite affordable prices. It is important, though, to check whatever items you find for problems like rips, stains, and the like, as certain conditions, such as severe discoloration or deterioration, cannot be corrected. Finding the true gem takes a good eye and requires patience, but it is well worth the effort.

Several years ago, for example, I purchased a used cropped midshipman's jacket in very good condition. I added ribbon stripes in white, navy, and gold to the cuffs and shoulders, and I pinned a handful of faux medals to the pocket—a signature piece was instantly born. I have worn that jacket year after year, and I still love it.

And owning pieces like that midshipman's jacket is the ultimate reward of adorning clothing yourself. Decorating well-made, well-fitting basic garments enables you to create a unique wardrobe, one filled with one-of-a-kind items that will outlast those fashion trends that too often lead us toward the costly and often unnecessary purchase of new clothing.

Although decorating basic clothing yourself has obvious financial merits, it also can be a very creative and enjoyable pastime. It is satisfying to create a design that reflects your personal taste. In fact, the techniques used on the following pages are so simple and effective that you will naturally begin to think of a variety of ways to apply them to your wardrobe. The pleasure found while beading a tie, for example, may encourage you to bead your own design onto a coat or sweater. You may find that you like weaving ribbon trimmings and want to apply them to all sorts of accessories—perhaps a belt, gloves, shoes, or a great hat.

Simply Sensational: Great Ideas for Buttons, Beads, Ribbons, and Lace will introduce you to many techniques for embellishment and inspire you to create clothing that is eye-catching, fun to wear, and cherished. Whether you re-create the garments shown on the following pages or use the ideas and techniques to create designs of your own, you'll find that it's easy to dress with individuality.

NOTES ON THE
INSTRUCTIONS IN THIS BOOK

It is assumed that all craftspersons using this book will have basic supplies—pencils, rulers, measuring tapes, pins, handsewing needles, scissors, and an iron—handy when working, so these are not listed in the materials lists. Special equipment, such as a sewing machine, is listed when it is needed.

•

It is important to note that the inch/metric equivalents in the instructions have been rounded up or down to facilitate the execution of a particular project. When working on a project, refer consistently to only one system of measurement.

•

It is always wise to preshrink washable garments and trims before beginning any decorative project; simply wash and dry them by the method you would normally use. Most trims are colorfast, but you should test them before applying them. In addition, remember that perspiration will cause some beads and sequins to discolor. Sequins should be pressed with care, as they may melt under a hot iron.

•

Each garment you decorate will be a different size and shape, so the quantities of trim specified should be taken as approximate guidelines. Your project may require more or less trim than the photographed sample. Take the time to measure the seams (or other area you plan to embellish) and the dimensions of your trim, then calculate the amount of trim you will need. Allow extra trim for easing, seams, and the adjusting of scallops or other patterns. There are notes throughout the text to help you make these calculations.

•

To keep the cut edges of ribbon from unraveling, coat them with an anti-fray solution. Anti-fray solutions are available at most notions stores.

•

When sewing beads in place, use only one strand of thread in the needle. Cut the thread in 12" (30cm) lengths and knot it securely when beginning and ending work. If you pass each length of thread through dressmaker's beeswax, it will be easier to handle.

•

When selecting the color thread with which to apply trim, use common sense. In most cases, your thread should match the trim. There are times, however, as when you sew on sequins in assorted colors, when it might be appropriate for the thread to match the background.

•

Use a slipstitch to apply ribbon or lace by hand. Pass the needle from the wrong side of the garment to the right side, piercing the edge of the trim. Return the needle to the wrong side of the garment, close to the place where it came up, stitching through the garment only. Slide the needle in the direction you are working and pass it to the right side, through the trim, once again. Repeat until the trim is secure.

SCOOP-NECK SHELL WITH RIBBON ROSES

The classic cotton jersey shell is extremely versatile. It can be worn with a casual suit, with walking shorts and a cardigan, or with a long skirt and flats, just to list a few possibilities. A shell is also a great piece to pack when traveling; it takes up little room in a suitcase, is virtually wrinkle-free, and is always in good taste.

Here, a scoop-neck cotton shell with cap sleeves takes on a dressier, more romantic look, thanks to the pastel ribbon roses handsewn along the neckline.

M A T E R I A L S :

- White scoop-neck cotton shell or T-shirt
- Large ribbon roses: 4 light pink, 3 light blue
- Small ribbon roses: 7 light pink, 12 dark pink, 6 dark blue, 33 white, 2 yellow
- Matching thread

D I R E C T I O N S :

Place the shell on a flat surface. Referring to the photograph and the Rose Arrangement Diagram, arrange and pin the roses along the front neckline. Pin two of the small roses to the hem of each sleeve. Sew each rose in place.

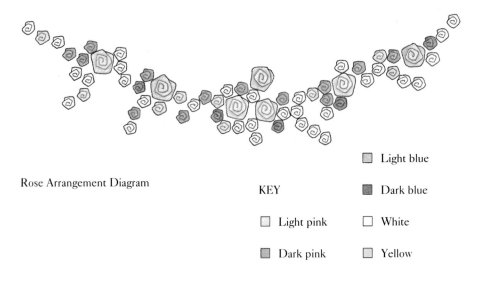

Rose Arrangement Diagram

KEY

☐ Light pink

☐ Dark pink

☐ Light blue

☐ Dark blue

☐ White

☐ Yellow

V-NECK SHELL WITH ROSE NECKLACE

You can easily dress up a plain shell—another wardrobe basic—with decorative trims. Here, the natural elegance of silk is enhanced by a delicate garland of ribbon roses. The colorful blooms match and contrast the turquoise silk and are accented by tiny seed pearls. If all of the roses were the same color as the background, the effect would be more subtle but no less beautiful; you might consider using black on black, or red on red. But you need not confine the shape of your design to the edge of the garment. For a chic personal accent, you might monogram a shirt or blazer by drawing your initials on the breast pocket and stitching small ribbon roses over the lines. For a romantic look, you could try scattering roses in an allover pattern on a simple sweater.

16

MATERIALS:

- Turquoise V-neck silk shell
- Small ribbon roses: 6 peach,
    7 turquoise, 8 cream
- Seed beads: one 1 oz (28g) package
    pearl
- Matching thread
- Silk pins
- Beading needle

DIRECTIONS:

Place the shell on a flat surface. Referring to the photograph, arrange and pin the roses along the neckline. Sew each rose in place. Using the beading needle, sew seed-bead pearls in between the roses; add a tendril of pearls to each end of the garland.

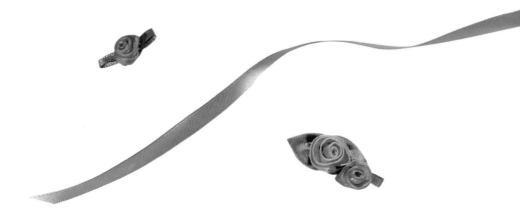

SWEATER WITH NEEDLEPOINT BERRIES

Traditional needlepoint requires canvas, wool, and a lot of time for the completion of a design. But this quick-and-easy technique makes it possible to capture the beautiful effect of needlepoint without the tedium, as it uses a charted design, and it substitutes ribbon for the usual yarn and the stitches of a knitted garment for the mesh of the canvas. Ribbon needlepoint (known to knitters as duplicate stitch) can be used to decorate sweaters, leggings, hats, mittens, and even knitted blankets. Here, a cardigan is bordered with a repeated berry motif; for other design ideas, look through knitting, needlepoint, or cross-stitch books for charted patterns.

> *The fabric of the sweater shown has approximately 4½ stitches in 1 horizontal inch (2.5cm); the berry motif is 9 stitches wide and 12 stitches high; as shown it is approximately 2" wide × 1¾" high (5cm × 4.5cm). If the gauge (the number of stitches per horizontal inch) of your sweater fabric differs, your berry may be larger or smaller, and may require more or less ribbon.*

MATERIALS:

- Light blue hand- or machine-knitted cardigan sweater
- Double-faced satin ribbon, ⅛" (3mm) wide:
  For each berry: approximately ⅔ yd (60cm) each pink and magenta; approximately ¼ yd (23cm) willow green
- Scrap paper for positioning berry motif
- Yarn needle

DIRECTIONS:

To determine the size of your stitched berry, mark a sample rectangle 9 stitches wide and 12 stitches high anywhere on your sweater; use straight pins to mark the perimeter. Measure the perimeter of this rectangle, and, from scrap paper, cut 16 rectangles with these dimensions. Mark the midpoint on one 9-stitch-wide side of each rectangle. Turn this edge so it is the bottom of the rectangle and cut a small notch in it at the mark; this mark represents the approximate position of the pink stitch marked by an arrow on the Berry Chart on page 21.

Remove the pins marking the sample rectangle from the sweater. Place the buttoned cardigan front-side up on a flat surface. Referring to the photograph, arrange the paper rectangles along the front edges, evenly spaced, with the marked sides toward the waistline, and pin them in place. (You may need to add or subtract paper rectangles to accommodate your sweater.) Unbutton the cardigan.

Embroider the motif on one side of the waistline first: to mark the first stitch on the sweater, place a pin through the knit stitch revealed by the notch cut in the edge of the paper rectangle; remove that rectangle. Don't knot the ribbon when embroidering; leave a short tail when beginning and ending, and weave the tails into the wrong side of the work when you are finished.

To embroider, follow the Duplicate Stitch Diagram and the Berry Chart on this page. Each square of the Berry Chart represents one stitch, and different color ribbons should be used as indicated. Work the pink and magenta stitches in duplicate stitch, and make long straight stitches for the green sprays. Thread the needle with pink ribbon, and begin with the stitch marked by the arrow. When the motif is complete, embroider the remaining berries in the same manner.

Duplicate Stitch Diagram

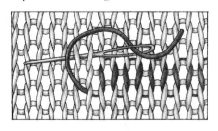

Berry Chart

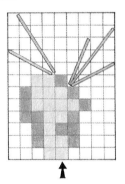

KEY

☐ Pink

▨ Magenta

▨ Willow green

RIBBONED BUSTIER WITH FOLDED ROSES

This floral bustier, with its clusters of lush hand-folded ribbon roses, is young, fresh, and charming. Paired with a pleated satin skirt, it is dressy and romantic; with jeans and a smart jacket, it is fun and informal. Here, the bustier is completely covered with overlapping strips of sheer floral-print ribbon; the translucent colors shimmer subtly. For a more sophisticated version, cover the bustier with a mélange of velvet, satin, metallic, and sheer ribbons in your favorite hue.

MATERIALS:

- Bustier
- Sheer ribbon, 2″ (5cm) wide:
    To cover bustier: approximately
        7 yds (6.4m) pink floral-print
    For each folded rose:
        approximately 1 yd (1m) pink
        or purple
    For each bud or leaf: 4″ (10cm)
        each pink or green, plus scrap
        of green for bud
- Cardboard tube or rectangle to wind
    ribbon onto
- Matching thread
- Pearl or crystal seed beads, for
    dew drops (as desired)
- Fabric glue

DIRECTIONS:

For BUSTIER

Folding the sheer floral ribbon in half lengthwise (selvages together), wind it onto the cardboard tube or rectangle.

Place the bustier, face up and waist toward you, on a flat surface. Pin the end of the ribbon to the lower edge, about 2″ (5cm) to the left of the center front; the folded edge should face the center. Unwind the ribbon, extending it diagonally to the top edge, just to the right of the center front, easing it over the bust as necessary. Pin the ribbon and cut off the excess. Slip-stitch the selvage edges of the ribbon to the bustier, making sure to finish the ends neatly.

Overlapping the stitched edge of the first piece by about ¼″ (6mm), position, pin, cut, and stitch another length of ribbon to the bustier. Continue in this manner until the bustier is half covered with ribbon.

Working in the same manner and reversing the direction of the diagonal slant, cover the remaining half of the bustier with ribbon.

Following the directions, make the desired number of folded roses, buds, and leaves. Referring to the photograph, arrange these pieces in the shape of a heart along the top of the bustier and sew them in place individually.

To sprinkle the roses with dew, glue beads onto the petals and leaves however you wish.

D I R E C T I O N S :

For ROSES, BUDS, AND LEAVES

For each rose:

Practice the following technique before cutting all of the ribbon into lengths.

Fold a 1 yd (1m) length of pink ribbon in half lengthwise; crease and hold it with your fingers. Refer to the diagrams below and on page 26 to fold the rose.

(1) Make a diagonal fold at the middle so that the two ends extend perpendicular to one another.

(2) Fold end A under and extend to the right.

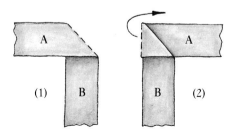

(3) Fold end B under and extend upward.

(4) Fold end A under and extend to the left.

(5) Fold end B under and extend downward.

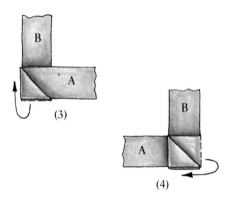

(3)

(4)

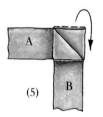

(5)

Continue in this manner until the length of ribbon has been folded into a square bundle.

Hold ends A and B between the fingers of one hand, letting the folds of the bundle relax. Gently pull one end of the ribbon through your fingers with your other hand; a series of folds will form in concentric triangles. When the size and shape of the rose are pleasing, secure the ribbon ends with a few stitches on the back of the bloom and cut off the excess.

For each bud or leaf:

Fold a piece of 4″ (10cm) long ribbon in half lengthwise. Twist it twice at the middle. Fold it in half at the twist, placing the ends together. Twist the ends, then wrap with thread and secure with a few stitches. Finish the buds by wrapping a scrap of green ribbon over the thread, twisting and stitching to secure.

WESTERN FRINGED JACKET

■

BEADED SHIRT COLLAR

A simple white shirt will shoot off sparks when you sprinkle the collar with crystal beads; fringe the Wild West onto a pristine denim jacket and you've made the perfect topper for your shirt. This fun outfit is easy to make. The beading takes a little time, but gets a head start with star-shaped gems. The grosgrain ribbon fringe is simple to do, too.

The fringe on this jacket is 6" (15cm) long and is made from ¼" (6mm) wide grosgrain ribbon. Before you begin, decide which of the seams on your jacket you wish to embellish, then measure each seam and add the lengths together. To make the fringe, you will need a total length of ribbon that is approximately 27 times the total length of the seams; this multiple applies whether you measure in inches or meters. In other words, if your seams are 40" long, you will need to buy 1,080" (30 yds) of ribbon; if your seams are 100cm long, you will need 2,700cm (27m) of ribbon.

M A T E R I A L S :

- White denim jacket
- White grosgrain ribbon, ¼" (6mm) wide: sufficient length for jacket seams, as explained in the box on page 27
- White thread
- Sewing machine

D I R E C T I O N S :

For **FRINGED JACKET**

Cut two pieces of ribbon that are the length of each seam you wish to decorate with fringe, plus 1" (2.5cm). For each inch (2.5cm) of this length, cut four 6" (15cm) -long lengths of ribbon.

You can pin the ribbon fringe together before you sew it, but this is not necessary. The easiest way to assemble the fringe is to place one long piece of ribbon and a pile of short pieces at your sewing machine, and to position and sew one short length after another onto the long one as follows:

Place the long ribbon under the presser foot of your sewing machine, parallel to the seam guidelines, with about ½" (12mm) extending behind the foot. Position a short piece of ribbon on top of and perpendicular to it, aligning one cut end of the short piece of ribbon with the right-hand long edge of the long ribbon, and sew it in place. Position another short piece of ribbon right next to the first one, aligning it in the same manner, and sew it in place. Continue to sew short pieces of ribbon onto the long one in this way until only ½" (12mm) of the long length of ribbon remains without fringe.

Place this piece of fringe on a flat surface with the short-ribbon-side facing up, and pin the matching long length of ribbon over it, aligning the edges. Using your sewing machine, sew the fringe and ribbon together along their long edges.

Repeat this process to make each length of fringe.

Sew each finished length of fringe to the jacket, by hand if necessary, turning under the raw ends of the long lengths of ribbon.

M A T E R I A L S :

For BEADED COLLAR

- White shirt with pointed collar
- Crystal seed beads: six 1 oz (28g) packages gold, three 1 oz (28g) packages white
- Crystal bugle beads: three 1 oz (28g) packages gold
- Six ¾″ (2cm) white crystal stars
- Faceted glass diamond-shaped buttons (optional): white to replace buttons on front of shirt, yellow to replace buttons on cuffs
- Fabric-marking pencil
- Matching thread
- Beading needle

D I R E C T I O N S :

For BEADED COLLAR

Fold the collar out and place it right-side up on a flat surface. Referring to the Collar Beading Diagram on page 31, pin three stars at each point, allowing space around each star for a row of bugle beads. Using a ruler and fabric-marking pencil, draw lines parallel to the outer edge of the collar to guide the placement of the rows of gold bugle beads.

Slipstitch the stars to the collar. Sewing through one bead at a time, sew on a row of bugle beads around each of the stars.

Working from the stars toward the center fronts and center back, sew rows of bugle beads over the marked guidelines.

Fill in the space between the two 3-row lines of bugle beads with densely spaced, individually sewn-on gold seed beads.

Fill in the space between the outer edge of the collar and the bugle beads as follows: bring the needle from the wrong side to the right side of the collar, pass it through five white seed beads, then pass it to the wrong side of the collar again. The spray of beads should lie smoothly against the right side. Continue to sew lines of five beads in a random pattern until the border is complete.

Replace the original shirt buttons with glass diamond-shaped buttons, if desired.

3 rows gold bugle beads

White crystal 5-bead sprays

Gold seed beads

3 rows gold bugle beads

Collar Beading Diagram

VEST WITH STAR CONSTELLATIONS AND BEADED TIE

Standard menswear has been sneaking into women's closets for some time—after all, it's easy to wear and conveys self-confidence. Why not give your tailored clothes a special glimmer of femininity with a sprinkling of beads or sequins? Depending upon your garment's fabric, these can be used to decorate a printed or woven pattern, like the geometric paisley on this tie, or to create a motif, like the constellations whirling on this solid gray vest.

Sew beads only onto the section of the tie that falls below the knot.

33

MATERIALS:

For VEST

- Vest
- Crystal seed beads: one 1 oz (28g) package white or desired color
- Matching thread
- Beading needle
- Fabric-marking pencil or tailor's chalk

DIRECTIONS:

For VEST

Map out real or imaginary constellations (on paper if desired). Use chalk or pencil to mark the position of each star (bead) onto the front of the vest.

Sew beads, one at a time, onto the marked patterns. Slide the needle and thread between the lining and top fabric when moving from one bead to the next; knot the thread securely at the beginning and end of work.

MATERIALS:

For BEADED TIE

- Tie
- Beads in colors to complement tie: two 1 oz (28g) packages each seed beads and bugle beads
- Matching thread
- Beading needle

DIRECTIONS:

For BEADED TIE

On the back of the wider end of the tie, release the stitches that secure the folds and open the fabric out. Turn the tie right-side up.

Sew beads, one at a time, onto the pattern that is woven or printed on fabric; knot the thread securely at the beginning and end of work.

Press the beaded area lightly with an iron, then refold the tie and resecure the folds with small stitches.

BEADED TOP AND BIKE SHORTS

Sporty exercise garb is great for working out, especially if you jazz it up with sequins and beads. Top a spangled duo like this tank and bike shorts with smart street clothes and you can wear it almost anywhere; think of adding a short, flouncy skirt and a satin baseball jacket, or letting the sparkle-trimmed neckline peek out from a white shirt with sleeves rolled and tails tied at the waist.

This outfit has been trimmed with rows of sequins and bugle beads, then finished with a fringe of hand-beaded bows; if you prefer, you could sew on purchased beaded or chainette fringe. When you sew beads or sequins to tight-fitting stretch garments, use short lengths of thread to attach just a few pieces at a time, and leave a small space between the end of one length and the beginning of the next. This will assure that your garment will still stretch as needed and prevent the thread from snapping, the beads from popping, or the garment from tearing when you are dressing.

Garments with beaded bows or fringe should be washed by hand or dry-cleaned.

M A T E R I A L S :

- Periwinkle cropped tank top and
    bike shorts
- Crystal seed beads: three 1 oz (28g)
    packages each white and royal
    blue
- Crystal bugle beads: one 1 oz (28g)
    package each white and royal blue
- Sequins, 5mm diameter: one
    400-piece package royal blue
- Matching thread
- Beading needle

D I R E C T I O N S :

Following the Beading Diagrams on page 38, sew trims to the front neckline of the tank top; sew on the sequins so they overlap. Follow the same diagrams to embellish the hem of each shorts leg, but place the bugle beads closest to the edge, then sew one beaded bow to the outside, above the sequins.

To make a row of beaded loops, bring the threaded needle to the right side of the garment, thread 8 royal blue seed beads onto it, and pass it back to the wrong side. Repeat this technique across the row.

To make a beaded bow, thread the needle and make a knot in the end of the thread. Pass the needle through 1 bugle bead, gently pulling the knot inside the bead. Follow the diagram, working in the direction indicated by the numbered arrows, to bead the bow. For each tail of the bow, use 1 bugle bead and 16 white seed beads; for each loop, use 18 white seed beads; for the knot, use 1 bugle bead and pass the thread through it as shown. When the last bugle bead is in place, finish off as follows: skipping the bugle bead, pass the needle back through the 4 seed beads above it and cut off any excess thread.

Beading Diagrams

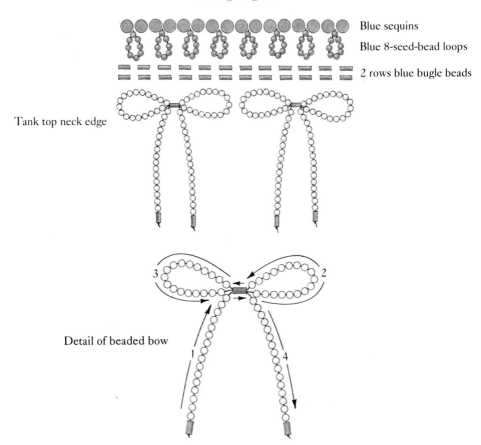

Blue sequins

Blue 8-seed-bead loops

2 rows blue bugle beads

Tank top neck edge

Detail of beaded bow

FAUX CUFF LINKS

There is such a marvelous selection of buttons available today that it could be difficult to decide which style to use for the chic cuff links shown on page 40. Fortunately, they are so easy to make that you can have as many pairs as you would like—raid the button box, check out the notions store, and keep a sharp eye at antique and thrift shops for gems from other eras. Button cuff links make great gifts, so it's a good idea to keep extras on hand.

FAUX MEDALS

Give yourself honors with a pocketful of these easy-to-make medals. Each medal is made from a short piece of ribbon, a bar-style pin back, and a button or button cover. You can use ribbon with martial stripes, as shown in the photograph on the next page, or choose an elegant moiré or velvet.

M A T E R I A L S :

- Two decorative buttons
- Two shirt buttons, 3/8" (1cm) diameter
- Two pieces narrow elastic, each 1" (2.5cm) long
- Matching thread

D I R E C T I O N S :

For CUFF LINKS

Overlap the ends of one piece of elastic and sew them together to make a loop. Flatten the loop, placing the seam at one end. Sew a decorative button to the seam; sew a shirt button to the opposite end. Repeat these simple steps to complete one pair of cuff links.

M A T E R I A L S :

For FAUX MEDALS

For each medal:

- Ribbon, 1¼" (3cm) wide: one piece 4" (10cm) long
- One decorative button or button cover
- One bar-style pin back, 1¼" (3cm) wide
- Assorted additional trims and other findings for embellishments: narrow ribbon, plain buttons, jump rings, elastic or heavy thread
- Matching thread

D I R E C T I O N S :

For FAUX MEDALS

Fold the ribbon in half crosswise, wrong-side out, and sew it together, 3/8" (1cm) from the cut ends, to form a loop. Turn the loop right-side out and press a crease at the seam.

Slide the bar part of the pin back inside the ribbon loop at the crease; sew the seam allowance to the bar. Turn the bar and ribbon loop so that the pin is on the back.

Referring to the photograph on page 40, tuck in the bottom edges of the ribbon loop to form a point; secure the point with a few stitches. Alternately, gather the bottom of the loop by wrapping it with thread or tying a smaller ribbon through it.

Sew a decorative button to the point. Alternately, sew a plain button, a loop of narrow ribbon, or elastic or heavy thread to the point, then snap a button cover onto it.

42

WOVEN EVENING BAG

■

BUTTON EARRINGS

When you create your own accessories, you can repeat trims and colors to coordinate them as you wish. Here, an evening bag woven of satin ribbon is closed with faceted glass buttons that repeat the bag's blue, pink, and mauve tones. The same buttons have been trimmed with strings of tiny gold beads and glued to earring backs; fancier buttons, like the gold-rimmed ones on the right, can go onto the earring backs without additional embellishment.

The bag is about 6″ (15cm) square, and there is no particular color-repeat in the arrangement of the ribbons, which are woven together in a simple over-one, under-one pattern. The braided shoulder strap is about 36″ (90cm) long.

MATERIALS:

- Double-faced satin ribbon,
  - ⅛" (3mm) wide:
    For purse: 4 yds (3.6m) each
      pink, cranberry, magenta, light
      blue, dark blue, and gray
    For strap and closure: 1¼ yds
      (114cm) each pink, light blue,
      and cranberry
- Fabric for lining: one piece
    12" × 6" (30 × 15cm)
- Matching thread
- Three rhinestone buttons, in colors
    to match ribbon
- Typing paper
- Masking tape
- Sewing machine

DIRECTIONS:

For EVENING BAG

Place the typing paper or interfacing on a flat surface.

Cut the ribbon into strips for weaving as follows: from each color, cut 36 strips 12" (30cm) long and 5 strips 6" (15cm) long; keep the two lengths in separate piles.

Selecting the colors randomly, arrange the longer strips of ribbon on the typing paper; the long edges should be adjacent to one another and the cut edges even. Covering as little ribbon as possible, tape the ends of the ribbons to the typing paper.

At one end, right next to the tape, weave a short piece of ribbon through the long ones: pass it over the first strip and under the second one; repeat across the row.

Weave a second short piece of ribbon next to the first, but begin by passing it under the first long strip and over the second.

Selecting the colors randomly, continue to weave in this manner until the long strips are woven together with short ones. Covering as little ribbon as possible, tape the ends of the short ribbons to the typing paper.

Sew the weaving together: place the stitches just inside the tape and stitch through the typing paper. Remove the tape and carefully tear the paper from the back of the ribbons.

Place the lining fabric right-side up on a flat surface. Place the weaving (wrong-side up, if there is a difference) over it. Pin and baste together along the edges, and trim any unevenness.

Sew the weaving to the lining along all edges; leave an opening for turning in the middle of one edge. Trim the seam allowance at the corners diagonally and turn the piece right-side out.

Press with an iron, then slipstitch the opening closed.

Angle the corners by poking each diagonally in between the lining and the ribbon. Fold the weaving in half crosswise (match the short ends) with the lining side in. Adjust the angles across each corner so that they match. Pin the bag together across each corner and down each side. Poke the bottom corners in to match the top ones, and pin the edges. Slipstitch the pinned edges to secure.

To make the shoulder strap, braid the three 1¼ yard (114cm) pieces of ribbon. Cut a 36" (90cm) piece from the braid, then finish the ends neatly and sew them to the top corners of the bag.

To finish the bag, sew the three buttons to the center top on one side. Adjust the remaining piece of braid into a loop to fasten around them, trimming any excess and finishing the ends neatly. Attach to the opening opposite the buttons.

For BUTTON EARRINGS

- Two buttons with shanks, if any, removed
- String of gold seed beads: enough to circle buttons
- One pair earring backs
- Glue gun and glue, or quick-setting craft glue

D I R E C T I O N S :

For BUTTON EARRINGS

Glue one button onto each earring back. Wrap beads around the perimeter of each and glue in place.

BEADED CAMISOLE AND TAP PANTS

■

CROPPED LACE JACKET

■

SATIN RIBBON PILLOW

■

CUTWORK PILLOWCASES

Pretty lingerie and linens are always lovely, yet they are too often luxuries that must be forgone. But with a little ingenuity, a bit of ribbon and lace, and a scattering of beads, you can create pieces that are worthy of a trousseau and perfect for shower gifts—or well-deserved indulgences for yourself.

To create lingerie fit to grace royalty, you can easily bead a special touch onto a camisole and tap pants—here the soft, figured fabric provides a motif to embellish—or you can quickly stitch a boxy lace jacket from a few yards of inexpensive trim. If you long for an elegant boudoir pillow, make one of pretty satin and brocade ribbons, or if your yearnings are for fancy bed linens, create cutwork trim by sewing lace appliqués to plain pillowcases then cutting away the background.

MATERIALS:

For BEADED CAMISOLE AND TAP PANTS

- Camisole and tap pants, of soft damask or other figured fabric
- Seed beads: two 1 oz (28g) packages pearl
- Matching thread
- Beading needle

DIRECTIONS:

For BEADED CAMISOLE AND TAP PANTS

Omit pearls from seat or crotch area of pants.

Place the lingerie on a flat surface and arrange pearl seed beads over part of the pattern in the fabric to create a simple but pretty effect. Your design need not be so complicated that you have to mark it onto the fabric.

Sew pearls, one at a time, as desired onto the lingerie, making sure to knot thread securely.

MATERIALS:

For CROPPED LACE JACKET

(Finished bust measurement is 38″ [98cm].)

- Ecru scallop-edged lace:
    4″ (10cm) wide for body:
       7¾ yds (7m)
    1″ (2.5cm) wide for trim:
       1⅔ yds (1.5m)
- Ecru grosgrain ribbon, ¼″ (6mm) wide: 4 yds (3.6m)
- Two small ecru ribbon roses
- Matching thread
- Sewing machine

D I R E C T I O N S :

Cut the wider lace into strips as follows: cut 7 strips 20″ (51cm) long and 14 strips 10″ (25.5cm) long; keep the two lengths in separate piles.

To make the back, place one of the longer strips right-side up on a flat surface. Align a second long strip, right-side up, right next to it; lap the edge of the second strip over the edge of the first. Pin and baste the strips together. Repeat until all the long strips are basted together. Sew strips together along basting.

To make half of the front, join 7 short strips in the same manner. Repeat to make the other front half. Sew strips together along basting.

Place one front half right-side up on a flat surface, with the lace strips horizontal and the last strip joined at the top. Matching the strips, place the second front, right-side down, over the first. To shape the neckline, at one top corner cut a quarter circle with a 3½″ (9cm) radius from both layers.

Place the back right-side up on a flat surface with the lace strips horizontal and the last strip joined at the top. Place the fronts, wrong-side up and neckline at center, over it, aligning strips. Pin fronts to back at shoulders. On each side, measure 9″ (23cm) down from shoulder edge; pin from this point to bottom edge. Making narrow seams, sew shoulders and sides where pinned. Press seams open.

To finish the raw edges, fold and press ¼″ (6mm) along center front, neck, and armholes toward the wrong side. Baste narrow lace along edges, covering pressed-under edge and easing around curves. Topstitch in place, finishing ends neatly.

Cut grosgrain ribbon into two equal pieces; tie each into a small bow with long streamers. Sew one bow to each side of neck at center front; sew a ribbon rose over knot of each.

M A T E R I A L S :

- One 12″ (30cm) square pillow form
- Muslin: two 13″ (32cm) squares
- Fabric for pillow back: one 13″ (32cm) square
- Assorted pink, green, and ecru satin, print, and brocade ribbons, 13″ (32cm) long: sufficient, with long edges aligned or overlapped, to cover one of the muslin squares
- Double-faced satin ribbon for braided trim, ⅜″ (1cm) wide: 2 yds (2m) each pink, green, and ecru
- Matching thread
- Sewing machine

D I R E C T I O N S :

Place one of the muslin squares on a flat surface. Arrange the assorted ribbons on it, aligning their long edges and overlapping as desired. Pin ribbons to the muslin and baste securely, then topstitch on long edges to secure.

Place the second muslin square on a flat surface. Place the fabric for the pillow back over it, right-side up, aligning the edges. Pin and baste along the edges.

Place the ribbon square, wrong-side up, over the pillow back square, aligning the edges and pinning them together securely.

Using a ½″ (1cm) seam allowance, sew the squares together; leave an 11″ (28cm) opening for turning in the middle of one edge. Trim the seam allowance at the corners diagonally and turn the piece right-side out.

Ease the pillow form into the covering and slipstitch the opening closed.

To make the trim, braid the three narrow pieces of double-faced ribbon; wrap them around the perimeter of the pillow, easing at the corners. Sew the braid to the pillow, cutting off the excess and finishing the ends neatly, or tying them in a bow at one corner.

M A T E R I A L S :

For PILLOWCASES

- One pair plain white pillowcases
- Two lace appliqués: if the motifs are not symmetrical, buy a pair that will be mirror images on the left and right sides of the bed
- Matching thread
- Zigzag sewing machine
- Tissue paper or tear-away interfacing
- Small sharp scissors

D I R E C T I O N S :

For PILLOWCASES

Wash and dry the pillowcases to preshrink them.

Place one pillowcase on a flat surface. Center a lace appliqué above the hem. Slide a piece of tissue paper or tear-away interfacing inside the pillowcase, under the appliqué. Pin and baste the appliqué through the top layer of fabric and the tissue. Repeat with the other pillowcase.

Set the sewing machine for a satin stitch that is wide enough to cover the edge of the lace appliqués. Stitch the perimeter of the appliqués to the pillowcases and tissue.

Tear the tissue away from the inside of the pillowcases. Carefully pull the pillowcase fabric away from behind the appliqués and cut it out inside the satin-stitch outlines.

SEQUIN-SPLASHED OPERA SCARF

One great scarf can really transform a sedate outfit into a knockout ensemble. Opera scarves—silky, long, and narrow, and usually lined and fringed—are available in all sorts of elegant and fun prints (vintage clothing shops are often a good source for wonderful old ones). Here, the swirling black-and-white print has been randomly splashed with bright sequins; depending upon the pattern on your scarf, you could concentrate the sequins at the border above the fringe, or use them to highlight special motifs.

55

MATERIALS:

- Opera scarf
- Multicolored sequins: one
    200-piece, assorted-sizes package
- Matching thread

DIRECTIONS:

Put the scarf on and look in the mirror to decide which areas you would like to decorate. Place the scarf on a flat surface and arrange the sequins on it to work out a specific pattern, if desired. Your design need not be so complicated that you have to mark it onto the fabric.

Sew sequins, one at a time, onto the scarf wherever desired. Wherever possible, slide the needle and thread between the lining and top fabric when moving from one sequin to the next. Knot the thread securely at the beginning and end of the work.

B L A Z E R   W I T H   L A C E   T R I M

■

L A P E L   P I N

If you have a plain blazer that seems to need a special touch, consider edging the collar and lapels, the cuffs, and perhaps even the pockets, with a pretty filigree of lace. A crisp white eyelet is very smart on a black blazer worn with a white shirt; you could use black on black for a more subtle effect, or ecru on any of the earth tones for an Old World look. For a different but equally sophisticated effect, sew another sort of trim—braid or passementerie, for example—to your jacket; you would probably want to stitch these on top, rather than behind, the edges.

You can finish off this or any other tailored ensemble with a smart pin. The one shown in the photograph can be made in minutes by gluing or sewing buttons to a bar-type pin back. (Use hot glue or quick-setting craft glue, and remove button shanks before gluing.)

> *To calculate how much lace you will need, measure the parts of the garment that you wish to embellish, add all measurements together, and add a bit extra to allow for easing and symmetry, seam allowances, and shrinkage.*

MATERIALS:

- Blazer
- Lace trim: sufficient to trim blazer as desired
- Matching thread

DIRECTIONS:

If your lace has only one finished edge, zigzag-stitch or bind the raw edge as desired before pinning it to the blazer.

Pin the lace under the edge of the collar and lapels of the blazer. Adjust the lace so that any scallops or other patterns fall symmetrically on the right and left sides, and seam it at the center back or notches of collar if necessary. End the lace neatly at the roll line of the lapels on the front edges.

Pin the lace under the lower edge of each sleeve, finishing the ends neatly. If desired, pin the lace under the edges of the pocket flaps (or inside the openings of the slash or patch pockets).

Handsew all the lace to the blazer.

BRASS-TRIMMED BLAZER

You need not look in the fanciest shop in town to find a dinner jacket as chic as this one, for it's just a classic blazer trimmed with dozens of bright brass buttons sewn in tight rows over the collar and cuffs. If you don't have a plain blazer that you'd like to embellish, visit a designer outlet or even a discount shop; the trim will outshine the quality of the blazer, so there is no need to start with something expensive. If you do want something with extra panache, search the thrift shops—you might find a smartly cut relic from the forties or a becomingly oversized man's jacket.

You can adapt this basic idea to suit your whim: choose rhinestone or pearl buttons for a completely different dressy look or assorted bright plastic ones for a fun effect. Buttons are heavy when massed as they are here, so choose a blazer with a sturdy collar and cuffs, or plan to sew the buttons in a single band along the edges. Thrift shops and yard sales are sometimes a good source of buttons—someone's abandoned button box can be your treasure trove.

Depending upon the size of your jacket and buttons, you are likely to need three to four dozen buttons per row. To determine how many buttons you will need, measure the length of the edges of the cuffs and collar of your blazer, and add them together. Divide this measurement by the average diameter of the buttons you plan to use, ¾" (2cm) for instance, to calculate the number of buttons needed for one row. Multiply this number by the number of rows desired.

M A T E R I A L S :

- Blazer
- Assorted buttons: enough to cover collar and band cuffs
- Matching thread

D I R E C T I O N S :

Sew a band of buttons at the lower edge of each sleeve. Space the buttons close together, working in rows as much as possible, but fitting smaller buttons next to larger ones as desired. Do not let the buttons hang over the edge. If your sleeves are lined, be sure not to pull the lining out of place when you are sewing.

In the same manner, sew buttons to the top of the collar: begin at the outer edge and work in rows toward the roll line (the neck seam). To ensure that the collar continues to fit properly, do not sew buttons on or inside the roll.

JEANS WITH LACE APPLIQUÉS

A small piece of lace can add lots of style to a pair of basic stone-washed jeans, transforming them from ordinary to unique in no time at all. One truly easy way to trim jeans is to sew a pair of lace appliqués to the front or back pockets, or onto the yoke, if there is one. Lace makes a great embellishment for other denim basics as well—think of adding it to an oversized jacket or even to a Western-style vest.

Look for lace appliqués in fabric and trimmings shops, or cut motifs from scraps of old lace curtains or tablecloths; if the motifs are not symmetrical, buy them in pairs that will be mirror images on the left and right sides of your garment.

MATERIALS:

- Jeans
- Two lace appliqués
- Matching thread

DIRECTIONS:

Referring to the photograph on the opposite page, pin an appliqué to the front of each pocket. Pin through the top layer of denim only, so that the pocket fabric is kept free. Sew the appliqués to the denim as pinned.

ANTIQUE LACE COLLAR

Antique lace fashioned into a simple collar gives a soft edge to a classic sweater or jewel-neck blouse. A fragile-looking lace such as this will drape delicately, but a beautiful, heavy piece could also look very elegant. You can often find pieces of fabulous old lace in vintage clothing shops or at antique shows (be sure to check for weak spots or bad stains). Fabric and trimmings stores carry many lovely new laces that may be less fragile.

This collar is made from two isosceles right triangles of lace that are joined along their long edges. You might start with a square of lace and cut it in half diagonally, or join several small pieces together. If you find a pretty lace that does not have nice edges, stitch a narrow lace trim to the short edges of the triangles before sewing them together.

Remember, all laces drape differently. You need not work with pieces the exact size specified below. Just wrap the lace around your neck to be sure it is flattering. You can tie or pin the finished scarf around your neck.

One variation on this look is a detachable Peter Pan collar. Simply buy a pair of crescent-shaped lace appliqués large enough to encircle your neck. By hand, sew them together at one end. At the open ends, sew a button on one side, and thread a loop to the other.

MATERIALS:

- Lace: two 20" (51cm) isosceles
  right triangles (the long edge
  should be about 28" [72cm])
- Matching thread

DIRECTIONS:

Place one lace triangle right-side up on a flat surface. Place the second lace triangle right-side up on top of it, aligning the edges. Pin along the long edge and sew together with a narrow seam. Turn the triangles so the seam is encased, and press with an iron.

LACE-TRIMMED NIGHTGOWN

Lace, whether it's a delicate, net-based sheer, a crisp eyelet, or a rich crochet, always adds a touch of femininity to anything it adorns. You can choose among many colors and textures to make yourself feel nostalgically Victorian, risqué, or prim—whatever your mood, there is a lace trim to suit it. Here, a wide flower-patterned white lace was added to a white nightgown. You might prefer a subtle contrast—perhaps ecru on white—or a striking one—black on red.

Lace can be easily added to the edges of plain garments like the simple nightgown on page 70, where it is also inset down the sleeves. You could also add lace to a robe, a slip, or a blouse. If you like to make your own clothes, you can incorporate lace into almost anything to which you'd like to lend a soft touch.

To calculate how much lace you will need, measure the parts of the garment that you wish to embellish, add all the measurements together, and add a bit extra to allow for seam allowances and shrinkage.

M A T E R I A L S :

- Nightgown or other garment
- Lace: sufficient to trim garment as desired
- Matching thread

D I R E C T I O N S :

Sew the lace to the edges of the garment by hand or by machine. If both edges of the lace are finished, you can sew it to the right side of the garment. If only one edge is finished, zigzag-stitch or bind the raw edge and place it on the wrong side of the garment.

To insert lace vertically on the sleeves, you must first remove the sleeves from the garment. Find the lengthwise center of each sleeve and cut it from top to hem. Sew the lace to the cut edges, finishing seams and hemming appropriately. (If the lengthwise edges of your lace are not symmetrical, you may wish to insert two lengths, adjacent to and facing one another, to make a balanced design.) Gather the sleeve caps and sew the sleeves back into the garment.

To insert lace horizontally on a garment, slash the garment where desired and refer to the preceding paragraph to apply the lace. If your lace is very wide, the garment will be longer when you are finished, so you might wish to cut some of the fabric away.

INDEX

A Appliqué, 53, 65, 66, *67*, 68

B Bag, evening, 43, *44*, 45, 46, 47

Beads, 10, 17, 24, 25, 27, 30, 31, *31*, 32, 34, 35, 37, 43, 50

Bows, 35, 37, *38*, 51

Bustier, *22*, *23*, 24, 25

Buttons, 39, 41, 43, 45, 57, *58*, 59, 60, *61*, 62

C Collars, lace, 66, *67*, 68

Cuff links, faux, 39, *40*, 41

F Fabrics, 12, 15, 17, 27, 29, 39, 48, 50, 52, 63, 65, 69

I Instructions

beaded tie, 34

bike shorts, 37

brass-trimmed jacket, 62

bustier with roses, 24, 25, 26

camisole, 50

cuff links, 41

earrings, 47

evening bag, 45, 46, 47

fringed jacket, 29, 30

jeans with appliqué, 65

lace collars, 68

lace jacket, 51

medals, 41, 42

notes on, 10–11

opera scarf, 56

pillow, 52, 53

scoop-neck shell, 14

sweater with needlepoint berries, 20, 21

tank top, 37, *38*

vest with beads, 34

v-neck shell, 17

J Jackets, 27, *28*, 29, 30, 48, 50, 51, 52, 57, *58*, 59, 60, *61*, 62

M Materials

basic, 10

beaded tie, 34

bike shorts, 37

brass-trimmed jacket, 62

bustier with roses, 24

camisole, 50

cuff links, 41

earrings, 47

evening bag, 45

fringed jacket, 29

jeans with appliqué, 65

lace collars, 68

lace jacket, 50

medals, 41

opera scarf, 56

pillow, 52, 53

scoop-neck shell, 14

sweater with needlepoint berries, 20

tank top, 37

vest with beads, 34

v-neck shell, 17

Medals, faux, 39, *40*, 41, 42

N Necklace, rose, 15, *16*, 17

Nightgown, 69, *70*, 71

P Pants

bike shorts, 35, *36*, 37

jeans, 63, *64*, 65

tap, 48, *49*, 50

Pillows, 48, 52, 53

R Ribbon, 39

grosgrain, 27, 29, 50

metallic, 22

roses, 12, 14, 50, 52

satin, *22*, 43

sheer, 24

velvet, 22

Roses, 12, 14, 22, *23*, 24, 25, 26, 50, 52

S Scarves, 54, *55*, 56

Sequins, 10, 32, 35, 37, *38*, 56

Shirt, beaded collar, 27, 30, 31, *31*

Stitches

duplicate, 18, *21*

slipstitch, 11, 24, 30

topstitch, 51, 52

zigzag, 59, 71

Sweater, 18, *19*, 20, 21

T Tie, 32, *33*, 34

Top

camisole, 48, *49*, 50

scoop-neck shell, 12, *13*, 14

tank, 35, *36*, 37

v-neck shell, 15, *16*, 17

V Vests, 32, *33*, 34, 63